To Be A Man

A Guide To
Manhood

Charles Sledge

Table Of Contents

Introduction

What does it mean to be a man? Different people have different answers, many would say it depends. That it depends on the culture, the time, and how things have "changed". They would say that manhood is a moving and changing thing. Something that adjusts to whatever the predominant beliefs or delusions of a particular society happen to be.

They'd say that manhood is something that has evolved throughout the years and now is something better and above all else different from what it was in the past barbaric ages. Others would say that perhaps there isn't even a need for manhood anymore. That it's a relic of a well forgotten age and good riddance to it. Now what it is males must do is make sure they do not contract this ancient some would say "toxic" disease.

And they'd all be wrong, dead wrong in fact. Manhood is not only something that has never changed and will never change. But it is also something that has nothing to do with the society that it's in. The principles that make up what it means to be a man though they may differ in their expression are the same across all cultures and traditions. And far from being "toxic" masculinity is needed and what all boys rightfully yearn for above all else. Masculinity is an unchanging powerful force that all males must learn to embrace, harness, and cultivate or be destroyed and of no worth.

This is the most important topic that a man will learn in his entire life. We live in a society where this much needed, this essential knowledge is considered at best taboo or even an evil that was supposed to have been eliminated. When it is in fact the opposite. Here you will be given the knowledge that you should have gotten your entire life.

This will fill the gap that schools, society, and unfortunately often family and friends fail to fill. You will learn about what it means to be a man and how this is a course that will change your life. It is the duty of every boy to become the man that he was born to be. Many die never seeing this, apply what is in this book and this doesn't have to be you.

The Spirit Of Man

What is a man? This is a question that many have attempted to answer. However few have answered this honestly and accurately. Most have their own agendas when it comes to defining what man is. Some wish to include the definition of man into their morality system whether it be religious or secular. For example I've heard a man is one who respects his fellow man or respects women and while in the right circumstances those may both be good things they have nothing to do with what a man is. Then there are those that address what a man is from an amoral stance and simply describe him biologically. There is good to this and these definitions have aided greatly in understanding what a man is.

However they still fall short of what a man is entirely. And truth be told what a man is entirely is something that is beyond the scope of a book. It is something deep and timeless. However something that has been left undescribed is what the spirit of man is and its importance in the grand scheme. Most males are disconnected from this spirit and therefore disconnected from their power. They have been led to believe in a multitude of lies and psyops designed to strip them of their virility and power. Those lies and psyops are a topic for another time and one that entire series could be written about. What's important here is understanding this spirit so one can get in better touch with it and overcome the obstacles of this world and age.

The Fire Within

Most males do not live with a fire within. They have been led to believe that masculinity is something that they can either joke about or is an evil. Those are the two options society gives (except for certain occasions when it's okay to be a certain definition of manly but only for a short time, for example during certain actions in war). However the vast majority of the time masculinity is either said to be responsible for the world's evils or a source of ridicule. These are designed to hide the truth of masculinity and to hide its power from those who have the potential to possess it. For the truth is masculinity is something sacred and powerful.

And like all things sacred and powerful they must be kept hidden and under wraps by those in power. This internal fire must be extinguished for with fire comes power. Fire casts out fear and allows one to use their own eyes in the darkness that has been lain upon the world. Anyone who wishes to keep those under their control in fear have to make sure that the fire never gets a chance to spread. But enough about others for this book and chapter are about you and your masculinity. The spirit of man is this fire within, this fire that animates one to life and to great deeds. It is available to all though some certainly make more use of it than others. Like the mind it is something that must be cultivated and grown.

Kings, Heroes, & Savages

This spirit is best seen in action. It is hard to describe with words and any word you use will fail to grasp it entirely. Even pictures such as fire does not do it complete justice. It is the spirit that animates great kings, legendary heroes, and savage warriors alike. It is what animates Alexander the Great to conquer the known world, inspires the Spartans to stand against the Persian hordes, and inspires many others like them. History is replete with examples of this fiery spirit of man and men who have cultivated it to great strength. It makes up the tales the one used to tell their sons whether of their ancestors or of great heroes of their tribe.

It can also be seen in the great myths and tales spun from a wise man's mind instead of from flesh and blood. It can be seen in both Achilles and Ulysses. As well as the tales of Conan the Barbarian and Tarzan of the Apes. Beowulf embodied this spirit to a great degree. As well as did great explorers whether they crossed the sea or went into uncharted lands with not much but water and sword or gun. As you see it's hard to describe this great, sacred, and powerful thing called manhood and masculinity. Yet when one sees it, it's impossible not to take notice of it. One mocks masculinity for the same reason one mocks God because they either fear it, don't understand it, or both. Or they know that their empire of deceit and destruction would collapse upon exposure to it.

Cultivate This Fire

The spirit of man is something that flows through you. It makes both the weak and the evil uncomfortable. It is something that must be cultivated and raised. It's vulnerable at first but eventually grows into the greatest and mightiest tree in the forest. Use others as your guide to start, that is how man as a species learns best. Then once you have a grasp of it you can grow it and use it in your own way. Expose yourself to it and you'll forever be changed by it. Don't fight against it or think of it as an evil.

You might as well think of the water you drink or the air that you breathe as an evil. It is your life force and life blood without water and air your body will die and without masculinity the same can be said of your spirit.

There are many ways to cultivate this fire. From books, to physical training, to bonding with other men. To suffering and coming out better on the other side. Going through the fire is an essential part of refining this part of your soul. The strongest of steel goes through the hottest of fire. The same can be said of manhood. The spirit of man needs to be cultivated and refined before it can be all that it can be. Begin this process sooner rather than later.

The 3 P's Of Manhood

There is a concept that has been floating around called the three P's of manhood. I'm not sure who first put it in this way though no doubt it (like everything else) has been around since time immemorial. While not perfect it does give a good glimpse of the tasks of man in this world and what goes into making a man a man. Now with that being said different people have used it for different ends. I commonly see the three P's put forth as a way for a man to serve women and children as if man was just a tool for women and children to exist and not that man was made for himself and his own existence.

Before I go further I will state the three P's here. They are as follows procreate (mate, attract women), protect (fight, defend), and provide (make money, collect resources). While there is certainly much more that goes into being a man that three P's do provide a decent base when used properly. Most put forth the three P's as ways that man can be useful to women, children, and society and that they have no further use than that. Though they don't often state this directly (that would raise red flags and rightly so) they imply it with how they address it. According to most man is a tool that varies in usefulness only to be used and discarded.

Obviously my version of the three P's is going to differ greatly from that of the mainstream. First off the three P's are there to benefit man himself and then those around him. A man has to put himself first even if he has wife and children who are loyal, good, and love him dearly. Still he must put himself first in order to fully take care of himself and by doing so take care of them. Regardless of what your goal or desire is you must put yourself first and foremost. This doesn't mean that you think less of others necessarily (though some you will think less of) but rather that you think more highly of yourself.

A Framework

Like I said above there is more to being a man than to procreate, protect, and provide or as I put them attract/mate, fight/defend, and acquire resources but the two A's and one F isn't nearly as catchy as the three P's. Though this is no all there is to manhood it is a good start and something that every man needs to master. Unless you are unnatural women will play a large part in your life either for pleasure or to bear strong sons and virtuous daughters, as well as to cook and clean and do other things you'd rather not do and are not suited for. Women are something that are either going to give you much pain or much pleasure depending on how you know how to handle them.

Then of course you must know how to defend yourself and your tribe. You may say that we don't live in a violent society so what's the point? But you'd be wrong on multiple accounts. First off mankind is violent always has been and always will be. Go into any neighborhood not of your kind late at night and see what happens. Mankind is still a violent and tribal species and always will be. To address this base level of being a man you must be able to fight off those would do you and those with you harm. Both hunter and warrior are the natural professions of man.

The acquirement of resources of also important. This can take many forms but in today's world they are all going to have to do with money. Unless you live on a self-sustaining farm (a noble goal and more power to you) however for most this is going to have to do with acquiring money. There is a "science" if you will of acquiring money that the masses do not understand (otherwise they'd have money). Understanding this science and gaining knowledge about how money works is fundamental to mastering the base level of being a man. The three P's.

Establishing A Base

Establishing a base, a strong foundation is important for developing anything and your masculinity and manhood is no exception. Like I said there is much more to being a man than the three P's but when it comes to your wellbeing and development they represent a solid base on which to build from. Handling them will allow you to go further and higher than before. They are the foundation upon which you can build more on.

Without a good foundation whatever is built will collapse in on itself. Your manhood is no different.

In this book we are going to look at ways to improve upon each area of the three P's. As well as how they relate to being a man and perhaps most importantly how men mislead themselves with each. A perfect example is a man who focuses solely on chasing women and sleeping with them and essentially sees himself as a human dildo. The more women he can sleep with the more of a man and the more worth that he has. Most would say this man is in error because he hurts women, but that is because they care nothing for men and only see everything from a woman's point of few (this includes the majority of men's writers). When in fact he is in error because he has placed women above his own manhood and development. He has put women above himself, something no man should ever do.

Not only am I going to show you the ways in which to improve every area of the three P's but also the fastest ways to do each. Then once you have these three areas covered you can move on to the more important aspects of manhood and masculinity. Something that very few males ever do because they are caught up chasing after one of the three P's never getting what they want from it or they place one of the three P's as their overall goal. The three P's are simply a base that once you get covered you start building bigger and better things on top. Even the greatest foundation just by itself is of little merit, it's what goes on top of that foundation.

The First P – Procreate

Alright now we'll dive into the first P of manhood. Procreate or attraction and mating. The general version of this goes something along the lines of a man's job is to reproduce, which is quite obvious if you ask me as it's the job of every species to reproduce. Above all else other than the desire for survival the desire for reproduction is going to be one of the strongest drives that humans have. Those who say otherwise are either very old, have hormonal issues, or lying through their teeth. I don't care if their a feminist talking about how sex is evil or they're a religious person saying the same thing or if they're one of those all women are evil and marriage is the worst thing ever whiners.

Look reproduction meaning mating and attracting the opposite sex makes up a large part of your life (if your healthy) and that's a good thing. The urge to reproduce while no doubt has caused many bad things but it is also responsible for many good things as well. Your drive for procreation is healthy and should be strong. So the first P of manhood procreate is going to come down to a couple of things. First off attracting a woman. Luckily what attracts women is simply a byproduct of being a man. Meaning if you're a man truly and fully then you'll have no trouble attracting more potential mates than you know what to do with.

You may sit there and think "I don't care about what women think about me or if they find me attractive, which makes me even more manly" when in fact you may very well be just a loser. Don't get me wrong a man should never live for the approval of woman but at the same time many are simply hiding behind that as a way to not address that they aren't much of a man and therefore not attractive to women. There is a difference between saying you don't care what women think from a place of strength and saying you don't care what women think from a place of weakness. One is good, the other is not.

How To Excel In This Area

Alright so first thing I'm going to address is the things that you can do to excel in this area. Remember first and foremost that women being attracted to you (procreation value so to speak) is in direct relation to your level of masculinity and anything that increases or enhances that. So things like adopting a more dominant frame is going to increase this, as well as making sure your testosterone is raised, as well as becoming strong and confident (both physically and mentally). I've written about this in nearly all of my books so I won't repeat too much here just give you an overall basis from which you can build.

Two areas that can use immediately improvement and help you dramatically are knowledge about how the mating game works (something nice guys and white knights even if built like Greek gods don't understand) as well as raising your testosterone levels as high as possible. Look guys with high testosterone attract more women and get laid more it's as simple as that. When it comes to the procreate portion of being a man testosterone cannot be beat. I know guys that can barely string a sentence together, don't know the first thing about "game" or bettering themselves, and pretty much have nothing else going for them yet get laid left and right and have women all over them.

And it's all because of the hormone called testosterone. Don't underestimate this. Getting your testosterone up is going to do more for this section of your life than every dating course and book in the world ever could. When it comes to the mating game, testosterone is king and comes first. The next thing that you can do but isn't nearly as powerful as raising your testosterone as well as without testosterone won't do you much good is learning about how the mating game works and in particular how being the "good man" society wants you to be turns of women like nothing else.

How This Relates To Manhood

Now there are a group of males who believe that any association with women is evil. They are the male equivalent of feminist. Many think that if you mention any aspect of masculinity and manhood in relation to women that you are cheapening it or betraying it but this is not the case. Man and woman were created for one another and balance out one another. Masculinity and femininity work together as yin and yang. Yes, one is dominant but they both play off of one another. I know of no man that would want to live in a world free of femininity and all true men enjoy and love femininity when it is expressed properly.

So don't think because the procreate portion of manhood has to do with women that it's somehow cheapened or that it's somehow a betrayal of "true manhood". Masculinity and femininity are related and play off one another in a unique, natural, and healthy way. Being attractive to women is not frivolous or "evil" as males who women have rejected because of their lack of masculinity like to claim. Rather it's related to a central tenet of masculinity. Biologically speaking the traits that make up masculinity are in general the ones that add to the chances of survival of a man and this survivability factor plays a major role in attracting women which is obviously needed for procreation to take place.

So women finding you attractive is often a reflection of the masculinity that they see in you. Being unattractive to women is more likely to mean you're not manly than it does that you're better than those that women find attractive. Now this can go in the other way too which I'll address in a moment the guy who bases his masculinity off how many women he conquers or pleases, which is another error. But I want to address their error of thinking rejecting women completely is either masculine or noble first. Because it's rank grow every day.

Procreation In Error

Alright so we've addressed how a key tenet of masculinity is being able to procreate and in order to do so one must attract women. The things that attract women are also the things that make one masculine and manly. We've also addressed how no being attractive to women is no virtue and is often in fact simply a lack of masculinity. We've also gone over how males who reject women completely from their lives are unnatural and not very masculine at all. Now we're going to cover the other side of the spectrum, the male who makes his largest goal in life to please women.

These two errors hatred and rejection of women and seeking to please women through sex have more in common than one would think. And not just because both are in error and failing to be men fully and completely. One thinks simply by not attracting women he is a man the other thinks that by attracting women he is a man. Procreation and thereby attracting women is simply one facet of masculinity and it largely stems from other things. Meaning that the things that attract women are the things that a man should be and do already. I'm talking about what truly attracts women not what society or women say attracts them which only weak males believe.

As I said this is simply one facet and isn't meant to define a man completely. Just like it's an error to tie up your definition of who you are as a man in a job it is just as much an error to tie up your definition of who you are as a man by how you "don't care what women think" or how many women you sleep with. This is simply one aspect of being a man that in our society gets way too much importance (probably because it's just about the only expression of masculinity left). Not sleeping with women doesn't make you a man, neither does sleeping with lots of women, but being attractive to women does. I know this can be very confusing but at the end of the day as long as you know that be a man and everything else falls into place then you're good.

The Second P – Protect

After procreate comes protect meaning to fight or defend. While the first P procreate is something that many males focus on and obsess over too much this area (protect) is something that is often neglected by many males in today's day and age. The ability to fight is something that has defined man since time began. Like I said man's natural professions are hunter and warrior both which require violence. Mastery of violence and being able to inflict it when it is needed is something that males were taught since boyhood.

Violence is part of life in this world and while it's unlikely that you'll get attacked by an enemy tribe now being capable of violence is still something that is important.

Those capable of violence are always given more respect both by men and women. It's something that is responded to on a primal level and therefore very powerful. Being able to fight is something that makes up a core part of being a man. You must be able to protect and defend yourself as well as your tribe and family. Even if you have neither tribe nor family. Even if you never have to face violence in your entire lifetime to be fully and completely a man you must be able to face it and overcome threats against you. We live in a society that is separated for the most part from violence but we are still the same humans that we were when we were breaking each other skulls with clubs.

Being able to fight not only gives you a sense of confidence (not bravado) in yourself that otherwise would not be there if you ever do need to call upon the ability it could very well save your life. A decade spent in the boxing gym is worth it if it keeps you from dying. One encounter with violence is all it takes to end one's life completely. Just because we are separated from violence for a large part doesn't mean it doesn't happen all around us. You have to be prepared for your own sake and for the sake of those that you care about.

How To Excel In This Area

Alright so knowing how to fight plays a part in being a man. It's not all there is but it plays a large part. My advice on this matter is going to be rather straightforward. First off I'd recommend you start doing a martial art of some sort. I'm biased towards boxing but different things work for different people. Just make sure it's not some McDojo with a guy who couldn't win a fight against a creaky board. Make sure it's legit and has application in real life. Meaning nothing fancy just tried and true practiced things that can cause damage and get the job done. The gym or dojo you choose will have a bigger impact (just about always) than the fighting style you choose.

You always want to pick up situational awareness (something that is just as likely to save your life as advanced fighting skills) as well as knowing what to look out for. Really this means keeping your head out of your ass and naturally scanning for threats and anything that seems out of place. In our modern society people get so caught up in themselves and bullshit that they don't notice strange things or put themselves in bad situations then end up hurt or even dead. Keep your eyes peeled and don't be a dumb ass.

I'd also recommend that you learn the basis of using a firearm. The laws of your country and state will vary but if you are allowed to carry one on you I'd recommend you do so. While learning how to use it and use it safely. A large part of this comes down to utilizing some common sense and not being a dumbass. Two things that are rare and always have been rare. How far you can take this is going to depend on the laws where you live. Follow the law and take whatever measures that you can to protect yourself and give yourself the best chance of never being a victim.

How This Relates To Manhood

So I covered this a bit in the beginning paragraphs of this chapter but I'll recap and add on some things here. A large part of manhood stems from biological programming. The three P's are no exception and all have to do with man's function as a biological being. Being able to protect oneself and fight off and conquer are fundamental aspects of what have made up manhood again since the beginning of time. Though society has changed what makes a man a man has not. I'll repeat that, though society has changed what makes a man a man has not.

This is why things like being capable of violence are more attractive to a woman than having a good investment plan. Sure in today's day and age the investment plan may be more important to survival but as a biological being it's the capability of violence that is triggering attraction in a woman's hindbrain. Other men also take notice of this and one's hierarchy within a group of males if often considered on those with fighting ability and the desire to use it. One who can knock another out with a single punch isn't going to get much gruff or fall low in the hierarchy.

Let's say that you don't care about hierarchy it doesn't matter. A strong man is a strong man. Regardless if he's the alpha of a tribe or a lone wolf sigma. The three P's and all aspects of masculinity discussed within these pages are important to being successful as either. Strength is tied to masculinity and the simplest and most undeniable part of strength is the ability to inflict violence upon your enemies. It is after all the basis from which essentially everything else stems from. Violence is power, this is undeniable. A man must be able to survive and even thrive in a violent world and the only way to do that is to be capable of violence oneself, even if it's only ever used in defense.

Protection In Error

There are two ways that the protect P of masculinity goes into error. One is through the male that would sacrifice himself without thought for things that are unworthy of sacrifice. The other is the male who thinks his fighting ability is his manhood and thinks that in the ring is the only area that has any merit when it comes to matters of masculinity and manhood both are in error and for different reasons. One believes that the act of sacrificing and protecting in and of itself and masculine and noble while the others things anything other than combat has no merit (and in particular his narrow definition of combat).

One is generally just an insecure bully and the other is either misguided or a coward or some mixture of both. We'll address the male who throws himself into the fire thinking that is noble. Sacrificing yourself for the sake of sacrificing yourself is not noble it is foolish, especially when you sacrifice yourself for something that cares little for you or is simply using you. This can be a country but I've seen far more examples of it being a woman. Males are taught to sacrifice themselves for women and women are more than happy to take advantage of this weakness in males. You must understand that sacrificing yourself is not noble and that protecting something unworthy of protecting is foolish. Protect yourself and you'll never go wrong, everything else has to earn your protection.

For those that think the only thing that matters is if one can beat them in the ring (and someone always can) their view of masculinity is very limited. Generally many errors (especially in the three P's) come from this, namely one is using their natural strength as sort of a cover for any weakness they may have. Some are naturally good at combat therefore all masculinity is defined by combat for them. Likewise some are good are attracting women and therefore all of masculinity is defined by how hot/many women are attracted. You see what I'm getting at here. Masculinity is a multifaceted thing, it encompasses far more than what one is naturally strong at.

The Third P – Provide

Now we come to the third and final P, provide. Provide simply means to acquire resources. At one time it may have been game meat, at another land, and now it's generally cash. While money isn't everything it sure is something and plays a role in how much you enjoy your life as well as your overall feelings of masculinity. While your job does not define you (something that is hard for many Westerners to grasp) it does have a huge impact on your life and your wellbeing. Most people work jobs they hate for a pay that allows them to just get by, some eventually upgrade to a job they hate with money to buy things they can't use because they're too busy working at a job they hate.

Nevertheless you need to acquire the resources to live some way. And some ways are certainly better than others. Ideally we'd all do something that we could make a living from that has to do with a passion we have but that's not realistic. But even if we have to work in less than ideal circumstances there are certainly ways to make it better and ways that are better for our masculinity than others. For example taking a pay cut but getting rid of a boss that is constantly nagging you and driving you crazy is going to be worth it. Getting better hormones from getting rid of the stress alone is going to be worth it.

So I don't want to get too caught up in a certain dollar figure here. Does that matter? Yeah, of course it does. Making six figures all else being equal is going to be better than not making six figures. But that all else is rarely if ever equal and it is that all else that can make a big difference. I'll use an example from a friend. This guy has worked as a marine biologist of some sort his entire life. Here's what his job consists off he pretty much spends all day hunting and fishing. I mean that's exaggerating a bit, but not by much. He's been offered promotion after promotion to go work an office job and make more but he turns them down every time because its one hundred times superior to what he'd be doing but getting paid more to do.

How To Excel In This Area

All of us are going to make money in a different way. However with that being said there are certain places where I would never recommend going as a man. The typical corporate environment being a prime one, anywhere that is dominated and controlled by women is going to be a living hell for a man unless he's at the top. The modern corporate environment is incredibly feminist in its leanings and promoting. The only place worse is the education system. There are some places in here where you won't be subjected to the asinine ball shrinking bureaucracy but they are few and far in between. Overall I'd recommend staying away from a corporate job like you'd stay away from the plague. And never work for a woman (you'll regret it).

So what does that leave? Actually many options. Here is a broad view of what I recommend at this time and that are going to be sane places for men. Law enforcement (this may change soon as the military has), fire fighter, entrepreneur, salesman, or passion based business. Again I see some of these changing in the near future. Now for how to excel in this area is going to be something that you can stand going to everyday (that's the first requirement) and is going to be different for each one (but not as much as you think).

Doesn't matter what you do you need sales knowledge, all sales knowledge is how to persuade humans. Doesn't matter if you're a LEO or whatever you need to have sales skills. There is no negotiating this. Sales skills and networking skills will get you far in any and every job. I'd also recommend copywriting and marketing (essential for entrepreneurs) no matter what your job as they both provide an in depth look into how humans work and what they respond to. As they say no matter what business that you are in, you're in the human business.

How This Relates To Manhood

A man is more than his job but that's a subject for a little further on. Providing for himself and for those around him has been the job of man since the beginning. A man who is dependent on others is seen as weak and not fully a man. While according to society (which in its natural state stems from biology) it is fine for women and children to lean on and rely on others, it's not the same for a man. A man who can't provide for himself or for his family feels it deep inside. Again it's biological. And it's something that a man has to master in his life to live fully and completely.

Especially now in such unpredictable economic times a man must do much to make sure that he can provide for all that he needs to provide for. He must make use of every advantage as well as learn all that he can about getting money. He can't rely on any loyalty from an employer not matter how hard he works, no matter how good he does. Providing for himself is something that allows a man to focus on other important things as well. Those without money can only focus on acquiring money. Because without none of the other stuff is going to matter for long.

This can be seen as the most fundamental of the three P's. Because without it none of the rest is going to matter much. Before civilization as we understand it failing in this P meant death because without resources one would not make it in this harsh world. While we will not die without resources now for men with pride it still represents a failure to them to not provide, because their biology is still the same. Meaning deep down their hindbrain is telling them that they're failing to survive. So taking care of this is an essential part of any man's life.

Provision In Error

Like all of the other P's of manhood there are many different ways to go in error with provide. I'll address some of the most common. The first is the male who thinks he is his job. I've seen this with jobs where there is some semblance of brotherhood (think military/LEO) which in one sense is good (the brotherhood part). But when it becomes one's sole identity and apart from their job they are nothing that is when it becomes unhealthy. Another is the guy who makes lots of money and then ties his sense of worth and masculinity to how much money he brings in. When his money goes his masculinity goes with according to him. Likewise if the other guy loses his spot on the squad then it's all over.

Obviously this isn't healthy or good. As I've said with all three P's. Procreate, protect, and provide they all make up facets of manhood and a healthy life they aren't manhood in and of themselves. Focusing on one to the detriment of others is not going to help you out. Money is important as is what you do for a living. But it is not everything and when you find yourself tying up everything to a job regardless of what that job is, it's time to take a step back and realize what makes up your masculinity. You are not your job. Your job is needed to provide resources and give you a avenue of growth. However the second is ideal only the first is a requirement.

Another mistake is to think that being a good provider allows you to go slack in other areas, it does not. Some males think that as long as they provide for themselves or their family then that's it and their all good. They fail to see that being a man requires much more of them. Providing is only a part of being a man, alone it does not cover it. Just because you can provide for yourself or your family doesn't mean it's all good and you can sit back because your job is done. That's not how it works, you must master all of the facets of being a man. Not one, call it quits, and then wonder why things didn't work out for you.

Masculinity & Freedom

What is it than men want most out of life? Depending on who you ask you'll get a variety of answers and truth be told there is no going to be one single answer this is after all a very broad question that will have to take into account a variety of factors. However with all that being said there are certain things that deep in a man's soul he yearns for. At first it'll be things he doesn't have it could be women/woman, money, or a number of other things. All good and all certainly part of a man's life. Yet I think there is something even deeper and that stays the same through all men and is intrinsically tied to what being a man is all about.

Some would say that this thing is power. Yet given the choice between ultimate power and ultimate freedom I believe that men would choose ultimate freedom. Granted with ultimate power you could have very much freedom and vice versa but you get the idea. And in this world if we have to make a choice most men would rather choose freedom. Let me explain as I have no illusions about the vast importance of power and push for all men to acquire more power throughout their life. Yet at the same time to appeal of freedom cannot be denied, though it's getting harder to harder to find in an increasingly unfree and regulated world.

When power impedes on your freedom too much it isn't worth it. I could be president of a country yet be miserable with all that came with it. The regimented schedule, not being able to simply breathe, and not being able to just take off and enjoy myself. Sure I'd technically have power (as much as my handlers would give me) but at the expense of freedom what's the point? I'd rather be a man with no debt, making an income that allows him agency and freedom to go where he wants and do what he wants than a man with great power such as a head of state or someone always in the spotlight. Granted there are those with power outside of the spot light (the one's with true power) I'm simply using this to illustrate a point. Power is no doubt important but so is freedom, if not more so.

Beware The Shackles

There are many different things that try to shackle men in this day and age (as every day and age before) from debt slavery to the emasculating culture. Everyone wants to tell you how you should think and feel and be. They don't want you to be free, they want you to be a good little slave that punches in the clock, thinks the right thoughts, and is emasculated enough to never question, never fight, and never go against the grain. Do all that and you'll be rewarded with an early grave and no appreciation from those around you. Drones are simply used and discarded, that is after all what they were manufactured for.

First off you must avoid debt. Some smart men can use debt to start a business and grow it much faster than they could otherwise. That's probably not you. You also want to avoid scams the greatest of which is college. For most of us it's too late and our priority should be paying off that debt and not getting into any more. Also you want to avoid buying a house that it's going to take you thirty or more years to pay off. Don't get things that you can buy. Rent a place or go small and live small. Again some of us are already past this point or this just isn't feasible. And our priority should be to pay down that debt as fast as possible.

Never acquire debt for frivolous things. Truth be told never acquire debt for any things but especially not for frivolous things. You want to be free and with debt you are never free, you are always a slave to your debtor until the debt is all paid back. Debt has become a normal part of our society, but just because something is accepted or even pushed by society at large does not in any way, shape, or form mean that it is either healthy or good. I can think of hundreds of examples of this, and debt is no exclusion. Treat debt as the shackle that it is, don't place it on yourself and if you're already caught in it do all that you can to break free from it.

The Deepest Shackle

But perhaps surprisingly the greatest and deepest shackle is not the one that is in your bank account or that comes every month. The greatest shackle is the ones in your mind. They are placed there from a variety of sources everything from what your parents taught you was right to your school to the media to your religious beliefs to things you've just picked up along the way. While many of these beliefs are good (don't run into the middle of a busy street etc.) others are not good and are holding you back stopping your development and even shackling your mind. Perhaps one belief you have is "Oh I'm poor/weak/a loser so I'll never be rich/be strong/be attractive to women" or some such other nonsense.

The shackles outside our mind are nothing compared to the one's within. Most males have shackled themselves into a corner, even falling for devious psyops designed to make them believe in their weakness. A perfect example of this is the elephant in the rope. When an elephant is captured for a circus or some other such matter the young calf is tied with a rope to a pole in the ground. The baby elephant fights day and night to snap the rope and escape to freedom but it's to no avail. Eventually after bloodying himself and even hurting his legs he gives up and gives in. He never again tries to break the rope.

That is why you'll see a full adult elephant tied to a pole with a tiny rope that he could easily break but he never will. That is because his handlers know that the shackles within his mind are much more powerful than the shackles without. The elephant remains in shackles even though all he would have to do is give a slight pull of his leg and the rope would snap with little effort. Like the elephant one must be wary of the shackles (limiting beliefs) that occupy the mind because they will cause the most damage overall.

Freedom

Freedom is what man desires. And while true freedom may be a thing of another place and time one can still maximize the freedom that they have in their lives. Freeing both their checkbooks and their minds is a good start. But it is not everything and freedom will look different to different men. For example to one male his ideal of freedom may be traveling across the country in an RV experiencing all that that this country has to offer, for another his ideal of freedom may be having a plot of land somewhere deep in the hills and country away from the degeneracy of civilization where he can live happy by himself or with his family, to another man freedom may be having enough income to rent an apartment in a city where he can expand his business and sleep with lots of good looking women. Every man is different yet every man desires freedom.

Every second you do not have freedom should be spent working to have freedom. Whatever burden you are living under you must free yourself from. A slave is never truly a man, ever. He may rationalize his slavery in some way whether it's debt, a job, a bad marriage, or whatever else but slavery is slavery. Freedom is what matters to a man's soul and will bring him what he wants. A man who is not free cannot be well and cannot be truly happy. Seek freedom and conduct your life in such a way that your freedom is never stepped upon.

The Natural Professions Of Man

Man when separated from his true self and what he was born to do naturally suffers. Just like if you plucked a fish out of water, it's not going to do well no matter how much work is done on it. Man is now separated from much of the things that brought him strength and solace before. Things like other men, nature, and close familial bonds. A man would hunt with his sons, defend with his brothers, and then spend time with his children before retiring and making love to his wife. Now this natural rhythm and natural way of living has been disrupted by many different things few of which are done for our benefit.

A large part of getting back in touch with your masculinity (something that more and more have never been in touch with their entire lives) in returning to primal ways. By primal I don't mean you need to throw out your shoes and forgo all of modern technology, that would be foolish. By primal I simply mean re-attuning yourself to how man has been throughout the ages. Man was not created to work in a cubicle all day and then go home to recharge so he can do it all again the next day.

There is much more to life than simply existing something that deep down every man knows.

There are many different ways that man seeks to reconnect with his masculinity. The use (and abuse) of the three P's are a prime example of this. Some guys feel that surge when they are closing a large deal or beating out a competitor. Others feel it through defeating another opponent in the ring or carving out another notch on their bedpost. Sure these things have value and represent something but I think there are even better ways one can reconnect with what it means to be a man and ignite their masculinity in a sea of androgyny. Though obviously the three P's whatever role they take in your life should not be neglected.

The Natural Professions Of Man

There are two natural professions of man as we would understand them. The hunter and the warrior. This may be a bit of an oversimplification but it serves as a good base from which to start. As we can see the protect portion of the three P's of manhood deals with the warrior profession quite largely. But it extends beyond that as well. For being a warrior is something that encompasses much more than one's performance in a ring where there are rules and regulations. Being a warrior is a way of life, as is being a hunter. I'll discuss what this means more in a moment. I just want to point out that there is more to this than most think.

Just because you do MMA and go hunting on the weekend does not mean that you are embodying these natural professions of man to their upmost extent. Don't get me wrong hunting is better than not hunting and fighting is better than not fighting but there is more to the picture. Like I said it's a way of life, a mindset if you will. Not that you're always looking to fight or see everyone and everything as prey. But I could go on forever about what it's not, it's best just to describe what it is.

It stems from an understanding of your nature as a man and your relation to this world. Man is born into this world that will often be against him. It is a test of his strength to see if he can overcome what nature has thrown at him. Can he overcome the long teeth of the lion? The number of the wolves? The famine that will strike? Or even worse can he withstand his most dangerous of enemies, other men? Being a hunter and warrior are the ways through which man overcame these challenges. Like I said they are a way of life more so than a job that is done for a set period of time then goes away.

Reconnecting Through The Natural Professions

Now if you've never hunted and never fought the first thing I'd recommend is that you do both. Do what works for you. You might choose one fighting style over another. You may choose going to the range over getting into the boxing ring on a frequent basis. You may go and shoot duck or you may track down big game. The point is to get out there and see what works for you and reconnect with this deep aspect of yourself and your masculinity. If you are a male that thinks these things "wrong" or "barbaric" then you need them more than ever. You might as well say eating, drinking, and reproducing are barbaric.

If you are already doing these things then take it a step further. For example for warriors read the biographies and works of great warriors before you. Get a look into their mindset and how they view the world and every day existence. You can also find what you can about great hunters though that will be rarer. A group of men that share many the traits of great hunters are great explorers which is another rich vein to mine. You've no doubt been told that these groups are evil men. As far as current society goes warriors who fight for themselves or a noble cause (other than globalism) are deemed evil as well as all hunters and explorers.

Another word of advice would be to stop listening to what mainstream society has to say on anything, especially on masculinity and what is good and what isn't. You must forge your own path using the wisdom of those who came before you and what you know is true deep down. What modern society deems wrong is often right. What modern society deems barbaric is simply natural, healthy, and masculine.

Don't let your enemy advise you on how to conduct yourself and live your life. And at this point in time society is no friend to man and masculinity.

Pain, Growth, & Challenge

If there is just about one thing that I guarantee you about this world is that you will suffer in it. You will experience pain and it will do its best to destroy you utterly and completely. Perhaps you think I'm exaggerating but I'm not. Your source of suffering will come from many different places. Some self-inflicted some just because it's the way that the world is. As a man it's your job to rise above this and for every punch you take to deliver two back twice as hard. You have to learn to get knocked around, have your teeth kicked in, yet still get up swinging because the world will have no mercy on you.

There is no such thing as fairness, justice, or mercy only weakness and strength. Once you live long enough you begin to see this. As I have said elsewhere when it really comes down to it, strength is the only thing that matters in this world. When you pull your head out of the little bubble of delusions that we all live in, this becomes quite obvious. Whining about the unfairness of the world is as pathetic as one who stays in their comfortable delusions. Like a ostrich sticking it's head in the sand hoping everything will turn out alright (it rarely does). A man must be able to look at this unfairness and this attempt by the world to crush him and laugh for he knows that he is strong enough to overcome it.

I don't mean to sound morbid either. I have no patience for either whining or pessimism. It's easy to just give up, cry, and whine and there are plenty of "men's" groups that will validate your crying. I will not. Pain is a part of life and this is good for it is through facing the world for what it is and overcoming that we become strong. For facing down the beast knowing exactly what it is and coming out the other side. For going through the abyss knowing what it is and coming out the other side stronger. It is not in man's nature to run, hide, or cry but rather to fight, go forward, and overcome.

"Good" Pain & Bad Pain

In weight training a good rule of thumb to stop training is when you feel a sharp pain. For example if you're bench pressing and suddenly your shoulder twinges you'd be wise to put the bar up right away and figure out what's up. Likewise soreness or pain of that sort is something you have to power through and something that will be a feature of your first couple of workouts. You simply have to suck it up and keep going. However if you kept going even when feeling sharp pain you'd injure yourself and you'd be a damn fool. There are those who think suffering for the sake of suffering is noble when it is not.

There is pain that causes growth and pain that was avoidable and is caused by foolishness. I'm not saying to seek out pain or suffering and wear it as some badge of honor. After all it's not the pain or suffering that bears merit but rather the overcoming of it. Any fool or jackass can experience tons of pain and suffering most of it self-inflicted. Growth is not caused by being an idiot then getting out of it.

Growth is caused by overcoming pain that comes from the world or regimented disciplined "pain". For example eating a strict diet over whatever you want, hitting the gym when you don't feel like, waking up at 6 to go for a run. Those are all examples of good "pain".

The point I want to get across is that it's not the pain and suffering that bears merit. It's the overcoming of such things. And there is certainly no merit in self-inflicted pain that comes from lack of wisdom and how the world works. Suffering for the sake of suffering or from stupidity is not virtue. I don't want you thinking that "Alright he said growth comes from suffering so I'll inflict lots of suffering upon myself and I'll grow a ton" unless that suffering is from discipline then it's not going to do you any good. Don't be a fool, the world will give you as much as you need and that's even if you're wise and knowing.

Where Growth Stems From

Now we'll address the type of pain and suffering where growth actually comes from. First off realize that with enough discipline and denial of baser instincts you can get just about anything you want from this life. Most just don't have the stones to get after what they want and therefore live their entire lives never knowing victory or defeat. They spend their entire lives on the sidelines and not in the arena. As a man our call is to the arena, and not just to the arena of life but to victory in the arena of life. In the arena we will be tried and tested and come out better, the world will throw challenges our way and we will overcome them for we are strong and grow stronger with every challenge.

This combined with our own training and discipline is where growth comes from. The challenges the world throws at us (along with the pain and suffering that brings) as well as through our own discipline and training ourselves for bigger and better things (with whatever pain and suffering that brings) both stimulate growth. Suffering because you're an idiot does not stimulate this growth, it simply shows you need to change your thinking. Also remember it's the overcoming of challenges that are throw your way and that you undertake that causes growth not the pain or suffering alone caused by these challenges.

Man is to overcome, to go forward, to grow, to fight, and to win. The challenges that cause the most growth are generally the one's that cause the most pain. We'll use two examples starting a diet and going through boot camp. The first while certainly good and can cause positive change does not cause nearly as much pain and suffering as the second. Yet obviously much more personal growth is going to occur through completing boot than from getting 12% body fat. As men we always need a challenge to face and another battle to win. This is good, natural, and healthy.

Men & Challenge

There is a great quote by one of my heroes General George S. Patton who stated "The more you sweat in peace, the less you bleed in war" which applies to what we are talking about here. Even if you are not in the middle of a crisis or experiencing a challenge that the world is throwing at you to fold and destroy you. You must keep yourself sharp. You must keep up your training and overcome challenges. Consider our own training we do ourselves as peace and the many challenges that the world will throw at you as war. To better face the challenges that will inevitably come you must keep yourself sharp and strong.

Not only that but you must be in a constant process of bettering yourself. Both your body and your mind training them both to serve you well. Become wiser and stronger every day. That is your mission, that is your goal, that is your purpose. When the barbarians are at the gate and you let yourself grow weak you and all you hold dear will be slaughtered. However when you have trained and prepared yourself for when they come they will be the ones who are slaughtered. Grow stronger, grow wiser, and be a man.

What Is The Measure Of A Man?

"What is the measure of a man?" is a question that has come up throughout history and one that just about everyone has an answer for. Different ideologies, religions, and peoples have said different things. Many of them echo one another, many of them are clearly for ideological or personal purposes, and others reflect things that are unique to a particular time, place, or culture and then there are of course some that are completely foolish and come from foolish minds. However nevertheless this is a question that has intrigued mankind for ages and one that seemingly doesn't have a consistent answer.

Most will tell you that each has its own grasp of the truth and while this may be true to some extent it is by no means the whole story. There is a timeless definition of a man, one that regardless of place, culture, or any other variable holds true and will always hold true. It is free of ideological poisoning or personal agendas or what one feels the definition of a man should be. The truth isn't always pleasant but it is the only basis from which one can base anything of worth on.
Ideologies are made to the be sweet

to the ears though they are poison to the mind and the soul. Just like what makes a man attractive to a woman has nothing to do with morality or ideology it's the same that what makes a man a man has nothing to do with morality or ideology.

The measure of a man is his strength. Perhaps you think otherwise. In this chapter I aim to not only show you that this is true but also to debunk the many other "measures of man" that have been proposed and that you may believe in. Measures that are often put with other goals in mind. For if you control the definition of something that gives you much power over that thing. For example if it's considered "good" to be a slave according to the slave master and the slaves believe it then it gives the slave master more power over the slaves.

False Measures

I'm going to address the first and perhaps most "traditional" (as we commonly understand that word now) view which is to measure a man based on a system of morality. Now I'm not saying morality is bad or anything of that matter. Morality certainly has its place and is very important when it is used in its proper form and when it's based on honor within a group not slave dictating to master. One can be moral without be manly likewise one can be manly without being moral. And as a matter of fact in today's day and age it can be hard to be both manly and moral if you use society's definition of morality. Manliness has its basis in biology, survival, and spiritually (though not morally) factors. For example one could be a good Christian (nothing wrong with that) give to the poor, turn the other cheek, and all of that yet he would not be manly though he was moral.

One may strive for both but the two should not be confused. There may (or may not) be rewards for being moral in the next world but there are not in this world. The next definition of what measures a man that is in error is that a man is whatever is useful to women and society. You probably hear women all the time spouting what the definition of a "real man" is (as if they had any say or clue in the matter). Or society talking about how a "real man" does the dishes, let's his wife screw other men, cuts off his own balls, etc. I'm exaggerating a little bit (but just a little bit) but you get the point. Society and women would redefine man as what is useful to them.

For society a man would essentially be a good slave. He tows the line, works his 40+ hours, let's his wife run things, gives his kids money to spend on consumer nonsense, has the required mortgage, and so on and so forth. For women their definition of man would be the exact same thing (a good slave, with a few exceptions for screwing). He'd be a guy who will support her delusions, buy her whatever she wants, give in to her whims, and allow her to get her sexual fill from a real man. And so on and so forth. Many males listening to society or women fall for this hence the modern emasculated male or the corporate drone. They are good slaves not good men.

The True Measure Of A Man

The true measure of a man is his strength. Nothing more and nothing less. While other things such as moral codes and certain ideologies can certainly add to a man's life at the end of the day his measure of who he is a man is based on his strength. It is strength that nature and reality responds to, nothing more and nothing less. Now you may be saying "But surely there is more to life than strength? Surely other things matter to a man than just his strength" and you'd be right. But we're not talking about living a full life here nor are we talking about living even an optimal life, what we're talking about is the measure of a man.

And the measure of a man is his strength. While other things may also be important to him. Things like morality, helping others, developing himself in other ways. He understands that underneath this all that his masculinity and manhood are judged by his strength and strength alone. Everything else is at best secondary to this first superior trait. So by all means develop other parts of yourself, expand, even be moral if you so choose. But understand that underneath it all the thing that matters and the measure of a man is his strength.

Because of this anything you can do to develop that strength is going to add to your manhood. And should take priority in your life. Strength is the foundation. The development of it and therefore you manhood doesn't have to take up one hundred percent of your life but when it comes down to it, it should be made a priority and take up a good amount of time and space. And by strength I do not mean simply just physical strength, though that plays a part. Also mental, spiritual, and every other facet of strength that there is. Remember strength is the measure of a man and as far as nature is concerned strength is the only virtue and weakness the only vice.

The Path Of Manhood

Something that I've talked about in other books namely *The Primer* is how while a girl will naturally mature into a woman just by aging and biology, manhood is different. A boy doesn't become a man just because he goes through puberty or hits a certain age. Manhood is something that a boy must be initiated into. It is something that he must earn and fight for. While as far as society is concerned a boy becomes a man on the age of eighteen or whenever he becomes of the draft able age, however many males will stay in a sense (the sense that matters) boys their entire life. Sure they'll grow facial hair, maybe have children, and maybe even on the outside look like a man.

But they will not be one. It's tragic but in our day and age there are many who die boys never having become men. And not from early deaths but rather from never knowing what manhood is and how to become a man. Through lack of knowledge and effort they don't become men. Many even if presented with the knowledge to become a man and the arduous path to manhood would shy away from it. For the path to manhood is not an easy one. It is one fraught with danger and hard roads. The path to remaining a boy would be like walking in a garden while the path to being a man would be climbing a steep mountain, with strong winds, and an enemy tribe occupying that mountain.

It's not for the faint of heart. But it's worth it, every step. The growth and pride that you feel in yourself cannot be replaced by any of the temptations of comfort and weakness. The path to manhood is choosing the harder right over the easier wrong. It's denying instant gratification for greater gratification down the road. So as you see these aren't things that simply come with age, have nothing to do with facial hair, and have everything to do with what's on the inside of a man (which the outside reflects at least in part).

The Path To Manhood

The path to manhood is growing and become better and better every day. I don't mean for this to sound like some shallow self-improvement trope. For this has very deep meaning. It's about ascending to be more and more day in and day out. About rising to be more and more. Truth be told it's not something that ever ends and not something that you accomplish and then don't have to think about again. It's not like a college degree or entering into a club. It's something that stays with you and is going to be with you forever more. Now I think I've described the path enough it's time to talk practical matters.

How does one become initiated into manhood? Especially without a tribe to do so? First thing I want to make clear is even with initiation it doesn't mean that one becomes a man as I've said it's a process and something that happens on the inside. Initiation is the beginning of the path, not the entire path. First thing is that becoming a man is an internal change and has to do with how you look at the world. You relation to the world changes when you go from boy to man. I never had an official initiation of any sort it was something that I grew into as I developed and learned. It was something I found myself becoming through overcoming challenges, growing wiser, and striving to be the best that I can be.

Wisdom and strength and two things that certainly separates boys from men (though they are not everything). Overcoming external and internal challenges will grow you more and more into a man. It's sort of like a skin that you grow into and then grow even more. Imagine you are filling a jar with water.

Overcoming external and internal challenges, bettering oneself each and every day is filling the jar with water. Most never fill even a quarter of the jar. Becoming a man would be like filling that jar. Then that jar once filled expands with the more water that you put in it. Manhood is a mold you fill and then it grows with you.

The Aspects Of Manhood

Man is not a one figured being. We've described him here as both a warrior and a hunter but that doesn't even begin to cover all that it means to be a man (though it's a damn good start). A man has many different aspects that make up his masculinity. There is the king, the savage, and many more. A man is the king of his domain and rules over it as a king should. Man also has a savage side used for his enemies to utterly eliminate and destroy all that would threaten him and those that are under his care. It's a multifaceted thing. You will grow in many different directions. Not everything will a confrontation of force or outsmarting an opponent.

You're strength (the true measure of a man) will be tested in many different ways. You will be tested physically, mentally, and spiritually. You will have to overcome weakness in yourself and overcome enemies. Some will come at you with their own strength, others will work through underhanded and devious methods. You must learn to fight the lion, the wolf, the ox, the viper, and the disease spreading rat. Not all your enemies and challenges can be overcome by the same thing. Your trials will share similarities with those who have come before and your brothers but they will be unique to you.

Brothers are indispensable as are mentors and ancestors yet when it comes down to it we have to walk the path of manhood on our own. Others will look on us and root for us, be by our side in certain trials, but at the end of the day we must stand on our own two feet and be prepared for whatever is around the next bend. Learn from the mentors, join with brothers, but stand on your own two feet. Constantly fight and constantly ascend. That is the path to manhood. We may never reach the summit of the mountain yet the strength, wisdom, and to earn our place among men from the journey is well worth it.

About The Author

Enjoyed the content? Then could you do me a favor? Leave a review on Amazon or tell a friend about the ways that the book has helped you. I love reading how my books have positively affected the lives of my readers. I read each and every review, they mean a lot to me. If you want to learn more I run a blog at charlessledge.com where you can find more content to further your masculine development to new heights. If you found value in the book drop by and join the community. Looking forward to hearing from you.

-Charles Sledge

Made in the USA
Coppell, TX
25 May 2021